What *Hell* Made

By

DANA BRADSHAW

I dedicate this to all those bravely facing the challenges of anxiety, depression, and addiction.

May these words be a beacon of hope, a testament to your strength, and a reminder that you are not alone. In the depths of your struggle, when the weight of the world feels unbearable, know that there are countless others walking alongside you, each with their own battles to fight.

It's okay to feel overwhelmed, to feel lost in the darkness. Your struggles are not a sign of weakness; they are a reflection of your courage, your resilience, and your unwavering spirit. Each day that you wake up and face the world, you are rewriting your story, painting a new picture of perseverance and hope.

Keep your head held high, even when the storms of life threaten to knock you down. Keep trying, even when it feels like you're taking one step forward and two steps back. And above all, never give up trying. Your journey to healing may be a long and arduous one, but with each obstacle you overcome, you are one step closer to a brighter tomorrow.

Lean on those who love you, who support you, and who believe in your strength. Reach out for help when the burden becomes too heavy to bear alone. Remember, you are deserving of love, of happiness, and of a life filled with purpose and joy.

As you navigate the ups and downs of your journey, may you find solace in the knowledge that you are never alone. You are a warrior, a fighter, and a survivor. Keep fighting, keep believing, and never lose hope. Turn your pain into power.

With unwavering love and support,
Dana Bradshaw.

TABLE OF CONTENTS

WHAT HELL MADE

From the depths of shadows is what hell made, she rose,
A girl with a spirit no torment could enclose.
Through abuse's cruel and relentless storm,
She found a strength, a fire to transform.

Death's icy grip brushed her tender soul,
Yet from its shadow, she emerged whole.
Humiliation's sting tried to dim her light,
But she blazed brighter, fierce in her fight.

Trust, once shattered, lay scattered in debris,
Yet she gathered each shard, brave and free.
Anxiety's whispers tried to hold her back,
But she marched forward, on a steadfast track.

In her eyes, a story of resilience told,
Of a journey through fire, fierce and bold.
She wears her scars like armor, unafraid,
For in the heart of darkness, she found her shade.

What hell made, she remade into her own,
A testament to strength, beautifully shown.
A girl who faced the worst, yet still she stands,
A survivor, a warrior, in her own hands.

Through the trials that sought to break her soul,
She found a strength, a purpose to extol.
In the face of despair, she chose to believe,

That within her, the power to achieve.
With each step, she reclaimed her voice,
No longer silenced by pain's cruel choice.
She spoke her truth, unafraid of the past,
For her scars were a story that would forever last.

In the mirror, she saw not just her face,
But the reflection of a survivor, a testament to grace.
She embraced her flaws, her imperfections bold,
For they were reminders of the strength she holds.

She learned to love herself, scars and all,
Embracing the journey, standing tall.
No longer defined by the darkness she knew,
But by the light she carried, shining through.

She faced her fears with courage in her heart,
Knowing that she had the power to restart.
With each sunrise, a new beginning she found,
Leaving behind the pain, on solid ground.

Her story is light for all,
Who face their own demons, big or small.
For in her journey, they see their own,
A reminder that they are not alone.

So, in the depths of what hell made,
She rose, unbroken, unafraid.
A girl transformed, her spirit ablaze,
A survivor, a warrior, in a world that she'll amaze.

BREAK THE CYCLE

In a world where dreams should bloom,
A girl's life shrouded in gloom.
Her father lost to drugs and streets,
A tale of pain that forever repeats.

Once a man with hopes so high,
Now lost in shadows, saying goodbye.
Betrayed by substances, by deceit,
Leaving his daughter's heart incomplete.

She longed for a father's love so true,
Guidance, warmth, a bond anew.
But fate's cruel hand dealt a bitter blow,
Robbing her of a love she'll never know.

Through tear-stained eyes, she sees,
The broken man her father used to be.
Memories of laughter, now stained with pain,
A life unraveled, never to regain.

She carries the weight of his mistakes,
A burden she silently undertakes.
Her path in life forever altered,
By a father's choices, once cherished, now faltered.

Yet in her heart, a flicker of hope,
That one day, with strength to cope,
She'll rise above the darkness of the past,
Embracing a future, free at last.

For though she's been robbed of a father's love,
Her spirit shines, undaunted, above.
She'll forge ahead, with courage, with grace,
A daughter of resilience, in life's relentless race.

She mourns the father she never knew,
His presence a void, a shade, a rue.
Yet in her grief, a resolve is born,
To break the cycle, to rise, adorn.

"Live by the sword, die by the sword,"
But she'll wield a different chord.
A life of love, of hope, of light,
In her, her father's wrongs set right.

For in her veins, his blood may flow,
But her path, her own to sow.
With every step, she'll choose anew,
A life that's hers, a life that's true.

LOST SOULS

In the depths of despair, where lost souls stray,
Yearning for solace, to find their way.
Their hearts burdened, by the weight of sin,
Lost and wandering, where to begin.

In the darkest of nights, when hope is thin,
God's light shines brightest, calling them in.
His favor and grace, a beacon so clear,
Guiding them through, dispelling all fear.

In His eyes, they're not forsaken,
His love unyielding, never shaken.
He extends His hand, reaching out in love,
To lead them home, to His arms above.

With each step they take, towards His light,
Lost souls find peace, dispelling the night.
His favor envelops, like a warm embrace,
His grace covers them, in every place.

No longer adrift, but found in His care,
They rise on wings, lifted by prayer.
God's favor and grace, a gift so fine,
Saving lost souls, with love's divine.

PEACE SHE FOUND

In the quiet of the morning, a gentle breeze,
Whispers of peace, rustling through the trees.
A soul once burdened, now light as air,
Finally free from the weight of despair.

In the depths of the night, a starry sky,
Glimmers of hope, shining from up high.
A mind once troubled, now calm and serene,
At last, finding solace in the unseen.

No more battles to fight, no more chains to break,
Only a sense of tranquility, a soul awake.
The past fades away, like a distant dream,
As the present unfolds, a new stream.

Embracing each moment, with gratitude and grace,
Feeling the warmth of the sun on her face.
A heart once weary, now full and light,
Basking in the beauty of life, day and night.

For in the journey of finding peace of mind,
She discovered the freedom of being kind.
To herself, to others, to the world around,
A newfound joy, in the peace she found.

Against All Odds

In the dead of night, from shadows, it whispers lies,
Filling her heart with fearful cries.
It wraps her mind in tangled vines,
A labyrinth of anxious signs.

Against all odds, she stands tall,
A warrior in a silent brawl.
With every breath, she fights the tide,
Refusing to let anxiety decide.

In the darkest hour, she finds her light,
A beacon of hope, burning bright.
She gathers strength from deep within,
A fire that burns, refusing to dim.

Through the storm, she walks with grace,
A survivor of the anxious race.
No longer in the shadows bound,
She rises, a victor, glory found.

Anxiety may try to claim her soul,
But she's a warrior, strong and whole.
From hell to excel, against all odds,
She rises, shining, a child of God.

ESTEEM AND SELF REFLECTION

In the mirror, she sees a reflection, a shadow appears
But it's distorted by her own perception.
A girl with low self-esteem, a heavy heart,
Trying to find herself, to make a fresh start.

She's been knocked down, time and again,
By words, by actions, by the pain within.
She's tried to fit in, to be like the rest,
But always feels like she's second best.

She looks for validation in others' eyes,
But all she finds are empty lies.
She longs to love herself, to feel whole,
To silence the voices that take their toll.

She tries to build herself up, brick by brick,
But self-doubt creeps in, making her sick.
She gets the dirtiest looks,
But the road to self-love is full of crooks.

She looks for happiness in external things,
But true joy comes from the love she brings,
To herself, to her soul, to her very core,
Learning to love herself, forevermore.

She takes each day as it comes, with grace,
Knowing that self-love is a lifelong race.
She celebrates small victories, each step forward,
Knowing that self-esteem can be restored.

She surrounds herself with love, with light,
Banishing the darkness, embracing the bright.
She learns that she's worthy, just as she is,
A beautiful soul, deserving of bliss.

In the end, she finds her way,
To self-acceptance, come what may.
She's a warrior, a fighter, a shining light,
A girl who conquered her inner fight.
In the depths of her soul, she digs deep,
To unearth the treasures she's meant to keep.
She confronts her demons, one by one,
Refusing to let them define what's done.

She looks in the mirror with kinder eyes,
Seeing her worth, dispelling the lies.
She embraces her flaws, her imperfections,
Knowing they're part of her unique reflections.

She practices self-love, a daily ritual,
Nourishing her spirit, making it habitual.
She surrounds herself with positivity,
Cultivating a mindset of possibility.

She learns to set boundaries, to say no,
To protect her peace, to let her light glow.
She leans on her support system, her tribe,
Knowing they're there to help her thrive.

She faces challenges with newfound strength,
Knowing she's capable, whatever the length.
She celebrates her progress, no matter how small,
Knowing that self-esteem is a journey, not a fall.

She embraces her journey, her lifetime quest,
To love herself fully, to be her best.
She's a beacon of hope, a testament,
To the power of self-love, to reinvent.

So to the girl with low self-esteem,
Know that you're not alone, in the stream.
Keep moving forward, one step at a time,
And watch as your self-esteem begins to climb.

A Life Without Trust

In a world where trust is fragile, she stands alone, in the
shadows,
A girl whose heart has turned to stone.
Druggings, abuse, rape, and death,
Betrayal's sting, stealing her breath.

She looks around with wary eyes,
Haunted by pasts, filled with cries.
Every smile seems like a lie,
Every kindness, a hidden knife.

She built walls, tall and strong,
To protect herself from further wrong.
She hides behind a mask of steel,
Afraid to show, afraid to feel.

She once believed in love and care,
But now those feelings she can't bear.
She walks through life with guarded steps,
Haunted by fears, by past regrets.

No one sees the pain she hides,
The scars that linger, the tears she bides.
She longs to trust, to let someone in,
But fear grips her heart, it's hard to begin.

Yet deep inside, a flicker remains,
A spark of hope, despite the chains.
She knows one day she'll find a way,
To trust again, to let light sway.

For in the darkness, there's always a glimmer,
A chance to heal, a chance to shimmer.
She's a survivor, strong and brave,
And one day, she'll rise above the grave.

Until then, she'll take it slow,
Letting trust bloom, letting it grow.
For she knows that healing takes time,
But she's determined to make the climb.

So to the girl who can't trust,
Know that you're not defined by the past's crust.
You're a warrior, a fighter, a soul so pure,
And one day, your trust will be the cure.
In the depths of her soul, a storm rages on,
A girl battered by life, yet to be withdrawn.
She's been hurt, she's been scarred,
But she refuses to let her spirit marred.

Druggings that clouded her mind,
Abuse that left her broken and blind.
Rape that stole her sense of self,
Death that took away her wealth.

Betrayal that cut her to the core,
Leaving her wary, forevermore.
She's learned the hard way, trust is a gamble,
A fragile thread, easy to unravel.

But deep down, she yearns to believe,
That there's goodness in the world, to perceive.
She longs for someone to prove her wrong,
To show her that trust can be strong.

So she treads carefully, with cautious stride,
Keeping her guard up, her heart tied.
But she's open to the possibility,
That one day, she'll find serendipity.

For she knows that healing takes time,
And trust is earned, not a dime.
She's a survivor, a warrior, a beacon of light,
And in her darkness, she'll find her might.

To the girl who can't trust, hold on,
For your strength will carry you through the dawn.
You're not alone, you're not defined,
By the scars of your past, by the bind.

Trust will come, in its own time,
And when it does, it'll be sublime.
For you've faced the worst, yet you're still here,
A testament to your resilience, your sheer will.
In the shadows of her past, she finds a glimmer of hope,
A reason to trust, a way to cope.
She learns to listen to her intuition,
To distinguish between genuine and illusion.

She surrounds herself with those who care,
Who understand her pain, her despair.
Slowly, she begins to let down her walls,
To trust in the goodness, despite the falls.

She takes small steps, testing the waters,
Reclaiming her power, her sense of quarters.
She learns that trust is a journey, not a destination,
A gradual process, a revelation.

With each act of kindness, each word of truth,
Her heart opens up, renewing her youth.
She realizes that she's not defined,
By the darkness of her past, by the confined.

She emerges from the shadows, a beacon of light,
A survivor of the darkest night.
She learns to trust in herself, in her strength,
To embrace life fully, regardless of length.

For in the end, it's not about the scars,
But about how she rose above the bars.
She's a testament to the human spirit,
To resilience, to the power to re-write it.

A Call to Black Men, A Single Black Womens' Thoughts

She's harder than ever, smarter than ever
And this world is cold, wet and rainy
and she's tired of the weather...

This black girls' magic
been raising the world,
always making it happen, she's tired.

She been working and feeding the family alone
its time for you black MEN to rise.
git up , its been far to long.

We need you to take your place,
take off them tight pants,
gold chains,
put on your boots,
get to work and come home,
Reclaim your throne!

RETURNING TO EARTH

In the deep shadow of what hell made,
A phoenix rises, from the shade.
Life after death, a true rebirth,
A journey of the soul, returning to earth.

From the ashes of despair, it soars,
A spirit renewed, opening new doors.
No longer bound by earthly ties,
It ascends to the heavens, to the skies.

In this realm beyond, where time stands still,
There's peace, there's light, there's a gentle thrill.
The soul is free, unburdened by pain,
Released from the cycle, the eternal chain.

It wanders through fields of endless bloom,
Breathing in the sweet perfume.
It dances with the stars, it sings with the moon,
In perfect harmony, in eternal tune.

It meets old friends, long lost in time,
Sharing stories, memories sublime.
It embraces loved ones, reunited at last,
In a timeless moment, the past is surpassed.

Life after death is a tapestry,
Woven with love, for all eternity.
It's a journey of the soul, a true rebirth,
A phoenix rising from the depths of earth.

So fear not the end, the final breath,
For life after death is not the end, but a new breadth.
A chance to start anew, to begin again,
In a world where love and light will always reign.

Beyond the veil of earthly life,
There lies a realm untouched by strife.
A realm where souls find their rest,
In the arms of the eternal, forever blessed.

Life after death is a mystery,
A journey into the unknown, a leap of faith.
But for those who believe, who hold onto hope,
It's a beautiful continuation, a true scope.

So let go of fear, embrace the light,
For in the end, everything will be all right.
Life after death is a new beginning,
A chance to soar, a chance to keep winning.
In the realm beyond, where spirits roam,
There's a sense of peace, a feeling of home.
Life after death is a transition,
A journey of the soul, a divine mission.

In this ethereal plane, time is fluid,
The past, the present, the future included.
The soul learns, it grows, it evolves,
In the infinite expanse, where everything revolves.

It connects with the universe, with all that is,
A part of the cosmic dance, in eternal bliss.
It explores the depths of its being,
Understanding, experiencing, freeing.

Life after death is a reunion,
With the essence of all, a divine communion.
It's a return to the source, the origin,
A merging of souls, a beautiful begin.

So when the time comes, fear not the unknown,
For life after death is a place to be shown.
A place of love, of light, of endless creation,
A true celebration, of life's culmination.

Until Now

In the quiet of my soul, a whisper stirs,
A tale untold, of silent battles endured.
No champion arose to fight my….. fight,
No love embraced me in the darkest night.

Alone I stood, against the raging storm,
No hand to hold, no shelter from harm.
In my flaws and faults, I found no charm,
Yet still, I longed for a love so warm.

Through trials and tears, I wandered lost,
In search of solace, of love uncrossed.
But time and again, my heart was tossed,
No one to love me, no matter the cost.

Until now, when a glimmer of light appears,
A love so pure, dispelling all fears.
Someone who sees me, beyond my tears,
And loves me, despite myself, through the years.

In your eyes, I find a reflection true,
A love so deep, so steadfast and new.
Finally, I'm seen, I'm loved, I'm understood,
For who I am, imperfect, yet so good.

No longer alone, in the fight or the flight,
For now, I'm loved, with all my might.

Until now, no one fought for me,
But now, in your love, I'm finally free.

DEPRESSION

From the shadows, a whisper, a sigh,
A girl survives, though she once wished to die.
In the depths of despair, she found her home,
But from the darkness, she has grown.

A silent scream, a hidden tear,
Depression's grip, a constant fear.
She walked through life, weighed down by sorrow,
But she found strength in each new tomorrow.

In the depths of her soul, a spark remained,
A light that flickered, that never waned.
She fought the demons, one by one,
Until the battle was finally won.

Through the haze of despair, she found her way,
To brighter skies, to a brand new day.
She learned to love herself, to be kind,
To leave the darkness far behind.

No longer defined by her past,
She found peace at last.
From the shadows, she emerged strong,
A survivor of depression, singing her song.

So if you ever find yourself in the dark,
Remember her story, remember her spark.

For in the depths of despair, there is light,
And you too can emerge, shining bright.

Empty Shell

In the depths of her being, a tempest swirls, shadow.
A girl battles demons, her spirit unfurls.
Years of abuse, neglect's icy touch,
Low self-esteem, a weight that's too much.

Invisible scars, etched deep in her soul,
Anxiety's grip, taking its toll.
She hides behind a fragile facade,
A warrior's heart, though it may seem flawed.

In the silence of night, she fights her fears,
Shedding silent tears, no one hears.
Haunted by memories, shadows of the past,
Each day a struggle, but she fights steadfast.

Through the haze of doubt, a glimmer shines,
A spark of hope, in the darkest of times.
She finds her voice, speaks her truth,
A journey of healing, from the days of her youth.

With each step forward, she grows stronger,
A survivor of pain, fear no longer.
From the ashes of despair, she rises high,
A beacon of courage, lighting up the sky.

No longer defined by her scars,
She embraces her strength, her battle scars.
A testament to resilience, a story to tell,
A girl battling anxiety, emerging from her shell.

In the shadows of hell, she dwells alone,
A girl with a heart that's turned to stone.
An empty shell, devoid of light,
Lost in the darkness, out of sight.

She walks through life with hollow eyes,
A soul that's shattered, filled with cries.
No warmth, no love, no joy inside,
Just emptiness, a relentless tide.

From the depths of despair, she cries out loud,
But her voice is lost in the silent shroud.
No one hears her, no one sees,
The pain that haunts her, like a disease.

She longs to feel, to be alive,
To break free from the shadows, to thrive.
But the darkness clings, it won't let go,
It whispers lies, it sinks her low.

She searches for a glimmer of hope,
A way to cope, a way to elope.
But the shadows loom, they're everywhere,
A suffocating weight, too much to bear.

She fights the demons, she fights the pain,
But it's a battle she cannot sustain.
She's tired, she's weary, she wants to rest,
To lay down her burdens, to be at her best.

But somewhere deep within her soul,
There's a flicker of light, a distant goal.
She knows that she must carry on,
To find her peace, to greet the dawn.

So she gathers her strength, she stands tall,
She refuses to let the shadows fall.
She'll break free from hell's dark spell,
And rise again, no longer an empty shell.

ANXIETY'S GRIP

In the depths of her being, a tempest swirls,
A girl battles demons, her spirit unfurls.
Years of abuse, neglect's icy touch,
Low self-esteem, a weight that's too much.

Invisible scars, etched deep in her soul,
Anxiety's grip, taking its toll.
She hides behind a fragile facade,
A warrior's heart, though it may seem flawed.

In the silence of night, she fights her fears,
Shedding silent tears, no one hears.
Haunted by memories, shadows of the past,
Each day a struggle, but she fights steadfast.

Through the haze of doubt, a glimmer shines,
A spark of hope, in the darkest of times.
She finds her voice, speaks her truth,
A journey of healing, from the days of her youth.

With each step forward, she grows stronger,
A survivor of pain, fear no longer.
From the ashes of despair, she rises high,
A beacon of courage, lighting up the sky.

No longer defined by her scars,
She embraces her strength, her battle scars.

A testament to resilience, a story to tell,
A girl battling anxiety, emerging from her shell.

NO LOVE

In the shadows, she learned to roam,
A young girl growing up alone.
No love to guide her on her way,
In the darkness, she learned to stay.

No gentle hand to hold her tight,
No warm embrace to ease her fright.
In the silence, she found her voice,
A strength within, her only choice.

She faced the world with eyes so wise,
A heart that's known too many goodbyes.
No love to shelter her from harm,
Yet she bloomed, like a rose, so calm.

In the echoes of her silent cries,
In the depths of her longing eyes,
No love to call her very own,
But in her heart, a love had grown.

A love for life, for all things pure,
For every struggle she'd endure.
No love from others did she need,
For in herself, she found the seed.

The seed of love that never dies,
The light within, that always tries.

No love to shape her destiny,
Yet she thrived, strong and free.

DRUNK AGAIN

In the haze of alcohol's embrace, a mere shadow A boy loses himself, his grace. Drunkenness takes hold, a vicious tide, Destroying his spirit, his sense of pride. He drowns his sorrows in a bottle's kiss, But finds no solace, only abyss. In the blur of each passing night, He loses pieces of himself, out of sight. His laughter turns to tears, his smiles to frowns, As drunkenness pulls him further down. He makes choices he regrets, His memory clouded, his mind beset. In the grip of alcohol's hold, He loses control, his story untold. His dreams slip away, his future unclear, As drunkenness whispers, "Come, have another." He wakes up each morning, filled with shame, Knowing he's the one to blame. Drunkenness has stolen his joy, his light, Leaving him lost in the darkness of night. But there's hope in the dawn's first light, A chance to break free, to make things right. He can choose a different path, a different way, To find himself again, to seize the day. So let his story be a warning, Of how drunkenness can destroy in the morning. But also a tale of redemption, of second chances, Of finding strength in life's dances. In the arms of alcohol, he sought escape, From the pain, the hurt, the heartache. But with each sip, he lost a part of himself, His spirit fading, like a book on a dusty shelf. He danced on tables, laughed too loud, Unaware of the crowd, That watched him fall, that watched him fail, As drunkenness wrapped him in its veil. He woke up in strange beds, with no memory of the night, Filled with regret, with a sense of plight. He lost friends, he lost love, As drunkenness pushed him, from above. His body bore the scars, his mind the weight, Of drunken decisions, of a twisted fate. He knew he had to change, to break free, From the chains of drunkenness, sobriety. To a brighter day, He had to learn to love himself, to forgive his past, To build a future, to make it last. And in his story, there's a lesson, Of how drunkenness can lead to regression. But also of strength, of resilience, Of finding light in the darkness, of breaking silence. So let his story be a beacon, For those lost in drunkenness, seeking freedom. In the depths of his despair, he found a glimmer of light, A reason to fight, to reclaim his right.

No Father Epidemic

In the shadows of our cities, unseen and unheard,
Lies a silent epidemic, a heart-wrenching chord.
Girls growing up with no guidance, no father to look to,
Left to navigate a world that can be harsh and askew.

Their fathers absent, for reasons varied and wide,
Some lost to prison, some to addiction's tide.
Some fathers simply never there from the start,
Leaving a void in their daughters' hearts.

Without a father's love, without his protective hand,
These girls face a world they may not understand.
They long for a father's wisdom, his strength and his care,
To guide them through life's challenges, to show them he's
there.

But in his absence, they find their own way,
Strong and resilient, come what may.
They learn to rely on themselves, on their own inner light,
To navigate the darkness, to emerge into the light.

Yet the impact of this epidemic cannot be denied,
It leaves a scar on these girls, deep and wide.
They long for a father's love, for his presence near,
To chase away their doubts, to calm their fears.

So let us not forget these girls, let us lend them our hand,
Let us be the fathers they need, the guiding hand.
Let us show them love and kindness, let us help them see,
That they are strong and capable, that they can be all they
aspire to be.

BEAUTY QUEEN

In a world of shadows, she stands alone,
A child of sorrow, her innocence overthrown.
Abused and broken, yet dreams still ignite,
In her heart of hearts, a spark of light.

She dreams of a crown, of beauty and grace,
A shimmering gown, a smile on her face.
To stand on a stage, in the world's keen sight,
To show them all she's more than their plight.

She'll wear her scars like diamonds, shining bright,
A testament to her strength, her will to fight.
No longer a victim, but a queen in her own right,
She'll rise above the darkness, into the light.

With each step she takes, she'll pave the way,
For others like her, who've lost their say.
To show them they're beautiful, no matter the past,
That they too can be queens, standing tall at last.

So watch her rise, like a phoenix from the flame,
Her spirit unbroken, her heart aflame.
A beauty queen, not just in name,
But in the way she inspires, in the way she'll claim.

Claim her throne, her rightful place,
In a world that tried to erase.

Ascension and Redemption

Finally, out of the shadows of a broken world, she stood,
A young girl, battered by life's cruel hand,
Her spirit dimmed, her heart misunderstood,
In the depths of despair, she made her stand.

Born into chaos, in a home of strife,
Abuse and neglect her daily bread,
Seeking solace in a dangerous life,
Lost in the darkness, her soul misled.

Darkness became her refuge, her escape,
A numbing fog to shield her from the pain,
But each hit brought her closer to the edge,
A fragile existence, teetering in vain.

Her beauty never faded, yet her laughter silenced,
Her dreams shattered by reality's cold grip,
But deep within her, a spark of defiance,
A flicker of hope, refusing to slip.

Through the haze of fog, she saw a light,
A path to redemption, a chance to start anew,
With trembling hands, she fought the endless night,
Choosing life over death, the hard road to pursue.

Healing became her battleground,
A war against demons, both real and within,
Slowly, steadily, she tore down
The walls of despair, letting healing begin.

With every step, she grew stronger,
Her spirit rising from the ashes of her past,
No longer a victim, but a survivor,
A testament to resilience that would forever last.

And when the time came, she spread her wings,
Ascending to a place beyond earthly pain,
In heaven's embrace, she found redemption,
Her journey complete, her soul finally free from chain.

Through valleys deep and mountains high,
She journeyed on, her spirit soaring free,
No longer bound by the chains of the past,
She embraced her future, whatever it may be.

Along the way, she touched many lives,
Inspiring hope where there once was none,
Her story a beacon of light in the darkest night,
A testament to all that can be overcome.

In the quiet moments, she remembered,
The struggles and trials that shaped her soul,
But they no longer defined her,
For she had found her true, authentic role.

With each sunrise, she felt the warmth,
Of a new day dawning, filled with endless possibility,
And as she gazed up at the vast, open sky,
She knew that her journey was far from over, in actuality.

For even in heaven's embrace, she continued to ascend,
Her spirit reaching ever higher, beyond the stars,
A symbol of triumph over adversity,
A reminder that no matter how far you fall, you can always
rise above the scars.

So let her story be a lesson to us all,
That no matter how dark the night may seem,
There is always a flicker of light,
A chance for redemption, a chance to dream.

www.ingramcontent.com/pod-product-compliance
Lightning Source LLC
La Vergne TN
LVHW051431080426
835508LV00022B/3344